Party of THREE ~

A Book About Triangles

by Christianne C. Jones

illustrated by Ronnie Rooney

Special thanks to our advisers for their expertise:
Stuart Farm, M.Ed., Mathematics Lecturer
University of North Dakota

Susan Kesselring, M.A., Literacy Educator
Rosemount-Apple Valley-Eagan (Minnesota) School District

PICTURE WINDOW BOOKS
Minneapolis, Minnesota

Editor: Jill Kalz
Designer: Joe Anderson
Creative Director: Keith Griffin
Editorial Director: Carol Jones
The illustrations in this book were created in acrylic paints.

Picture Window Books
5115 Excelsior Boulevard
Suite 232
Minneapolis, MN 55416
877-845-8392
www.picturewindowbooks.com

Printed in the United States of America.

Library of Congress Cataloging-in-Publication Data
Jones, Christianne C.
Party of three : a book about triangles / by Christianne C. Jones ; illustrated by Ronnie Rooney.
p. cm. – (Know your shapes)
Includes bibliographical references and index.
ISBN 1-4048-1575-9
1. Triangle–Juvenile literature. I. Rooney, Ronnie, ill. II. Title.
QA482.J663 2006
516'.154–dc22
2005021845

Shapes are all around. You can find them everywhere you look. Shapes can be tall and skinny, short and round, long and wide. Some shapes will look the same, and some will look different, but they are all amazing.
Let's find some shapes!

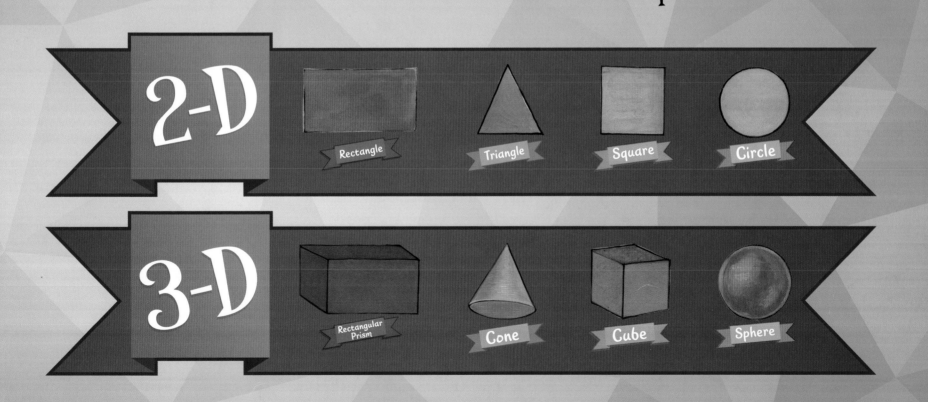

2-D

Rectangle   Triangle   Square   Circle

3-D

Rectangular Prism   Cone   Cube   Sphere

They have three corners and three sides. Where do triangles like to hide?

Flapping triangles decorate my house.

A cheesy triangle
belongs to this mouse.

8

Hot triangles
make us grin.

10

Skinny triangles
are fun to pin.

12

Sweet triangles drip in the heat.

Folded triangles keep us neat.

16

Paper triangles
sit on our heads.

Warm, blue triangles cover my bed.

The party is over, and here comes the moon. Do you see other triangles in my room?

23

MUSICAL TRIANGLE

WHAT YOU NEED:
- A metal clothes hanger
- A piece of yarn or string
- A spoon

WHAT YOU DO:
1. Have an adult bend the hanger hook to make a complete circle.
2. Tie the piece of yarn or string to the circle.
3. Hold the triangle by the yarn or string.
4. Hit the sides of the triangle with the spoon to make fun, musical sounds!

LOOK FOR ALL OF THE BOOKS IN THE KNOW YOUR SHAPES SERIES:
Around the Park: A Book About Circles 1-4048-1572-4
Four Sides the Same: A Book About Squares 1-4048-1574-0
Party of Three: A Book About Triangles 1-4048-1575-9
Two Short, Two Long: A Book About Rectangles 1-4048-1573-2

FUN FACTS

► Two-dimensional (2-D) shapes are flat. They have just a front and a back. Three-dimensional (3-D) shapes have a front, a back, and sides. A cone is a 3-D triangle.

► Ice cream cones are a common treat in the United States. Vanilla is the most popular ice cream flavor. Chocolate is the second most popular flavor.

► The average American eats six slices of pie each year.

TO LEARN MORE

AT THE LIBRARY
Bruce, Lisa. *Patterns in the Park.* Chicago: Raintree, 2004.
Burke, Jennifer S. *Triangles.* New York: Children's Press, 2000.
Schuette, Sarah L. *Triangles.* Mankato, Minn.: A+ Books, 2003.
Scott, Janine. *The Shapes of Things.* Minneapolis: Compass Point Books, 2003.

ON THE WEB
FactHound offers a safe, fun way to find Internet sites related to this book. All of the sites on FactHound have been researched by our staff.
1. Visit www.facthound.com
2. Type in this special code for age-appropriate sites: 1404815759
3. Click on the FETCH IT button.
Your trusty FactHound will fetch the best sites for you!